FINDING
GREATNESS
FROM WITHIN

AN ETHOS

FOR A BETTER TOMORROW

BY
ALONSO SANCHEZ

FINDING GREATNESS FROM WITHIN

ALONSO SANCHEZ

"Warriors are not what you think of as warriors. The warrior is not someone who fights, because no one has the right to take another life. The warrior, for us, is one who sacrifices himself for the good of others. His task is to take care of the elderly, the defenseless, those who cannot provide for themselves, and above all, the children, the future of humanity."

-Sitting Bull

Ethos is a Greek word meaning "character" that is used to describe the guiding beliefs or ideals that characterize a community, nation or ideology. *(Wikipedia)*

The Marine Corp's core values of Honor, Courage, and Commitment have gained increased prominence in recent years. This "warrior **ethos**" provides guidance to Marines in difficult ethical situations and acts as a reminder to provide good order and discipline. *(Google)*

The warrior ethos is a code of conduct that embodies a life where **integrity**, loyalty, honor, selflessness and **courage** are one›s guide. (Pressfield Gazette/ book review)

1. They always put the Mission First

2. They never accept Defeat

3. They never leave a Fallen Comrade.

I fell in love with this creed, the unity and brotherhood that they share among themselves is truly inspiring. They live by a code and they die by that code. In our normal everyday world it would be great if we all lived in a way that modeled the U.S. Marine ethos instead of everyone for themselves mentally. I believe that if we all had a common goal and a code of conduct we would do so much better as human race. I wanted to share a set of beliefs that I learned in my yoga teacher training that empowers others and yourself to make a difference. I am taking this opportunity to share what I have heard and learned to inspire you to create your own ethos.

MY ETHOS:

1. People - Planet - Profit should be our mission and always put people first 'Simon Snek'

2. Stand together to never accept defeat in any aspect of our lives.

3. We all bleed red blood; never turn our backs on each other.

Let's impact change in the lives of everyone we meet.

––––––––––––

ALONSO SANCHEZ
www.alonsosanchez.com

My goal with this book is to inspire and empower you to strive for greatness. All of these thoughts are in no particular order, and they are the questions or statements I ask myself. I made this book in a format so that you can interact and journal on each thought if it triggers you or if you get inspired by it. All the quotes in this book personally touched my soul.

1. Start each day with a CLEAR intention, each new day brings new opportunities.

_____

_____

_____

_____

_____

_____

_____

_____

_____

_____

_____

_____

_____

_____

_____

_____

_____

_____

_____

Remember this: our feelings are not a choice; our behavior and our thoughts are always a choice. Choose to evolve, to impact change. It's never too late to make a difference in your life or the life of another person.

-Alonso Sanchez

2. Completing the 1st task of the day sets a tone for the rest of your day. Each day, take a moment and make your bed. (Navy Admiral William H. McRaven) I heard his 2014 Commencement Address to the graduating class. His speech made a huge impact in my life.

_____

_____

_____

_____

_____

_____

_____

_____

_____

_____

_____

_____

_____

_____

_____

_____

_____

The greatest danger for most of us is not that our aim is too high and we miss it, but that it is too low and we reach it.

———————

-Michelangelo

"Empty your mind, be formless, shapeless, like water. If you put water into a cup, it becomes the cup. You put water in a bottle and it becomes the bottle. You put it in a teapot it becomes the teapot. Now, water can flow or it can crash. Be water my friend."

-Bruce Lee

3. Appreciate everything and everyone in your life, be grateful, be kind, and show gratitude.

_____

_____

_____

_____

_____

_____

_____

_____

_____

_____

_____

_____

_____

_____

_____

_____

_____

Courage doesn't always roar, sometimes courage is the quiet voice at the end of the day saying, I will try again tomorrow."

-Mary Anne Redmacher

4. Show empathy and compassion to others. We have the ability to understand, to share and to show emotions to others. Blocking emotions creates anger inside, which consumes your every thought and it doesn't allow you to grow.

_____

_____

_____

_____

_____

_____

_____

_____

_____

_____

_____

_____

_____

_____

_____

_____

_____

_____

_____

_____

_____

_____

I used to think the worst thing in life was to end up all alone. It's not, the worst thing in life is to end up with people who make you feel all alone.

-Robin Williams

"Be careful what you think about because you will surely get it!"

- Thomas Carlisle

5. Stop blaming others for your failures and shortcomings, take responsibility and own up to your mistakes. Learn from them to make yourself a better version of how you were yesterday.

_____

_____

_____

_____

_____

_____

_____

_____

_____

_____

_____

_____

_____

_____

_____

_____

_____

_____

_____

_____

"If I believe I cannot do something, it makes me incapable of doing it. But when I believe I can, I acquire the ability to do it, even if I did not have the ability in the beginning!"

-Mahatma Gandhi

6. At the beginning of each new day you have a new opportunity to do something new; yesterday you told yourself today was the day. Go out and seize the day!

_____

_____

_____

_____

_____

_____

_____

_____

_____

_____

_____

_____

_____

_____

_____

_____

_____

_____

_____

"Too many people spend money they haven't earned, to buy things they don't want, to impress people they don't like."

-Will Smith

"If you know the enemy better than you know yourself the outcome of the battle has already been decided."

-Sun Tzu "The Art of War"

7. With every transformation you will encounter that it will be worse before it gets better; that is a huge part of personal growth. On the other side of pain you will encounter greatness.

_____

_____

_____

_____

_____

_____

_____

_____

_____

_____

_____

_____

_____

_____

_____

_____

_____

_____

_____

"If you change the way you look at things, the things you look at change."

-Dr. Wayne Dryer

8. Setting your goals for your life intentions is your road map to success, without them how can you expect to reach your destination? Take a moment and write down a few goals you want to achieve, it all starts with a thought to be able to make them a reality.

_____

_____

_____

_____

_____

_____

_____

_____

_____

_____

_____

_____

_____

_____

_____

_____

_____

_____

"If you do what you've always done, you'll get what you've always gotten."

-Tony Robbins

"My soul is not contained within the limits of my body; my body is contained within the limitlessness of my soul."

-Jim Carrey

9. Visualization is one of the most important tools we underutilize. Visualize your goals, grind towards them daily. You must want them more than life itself and watch how they become your reality.

_____

_____

_____

_____

_____

_____

_____

_____

_____

_____

_____

_____

_____

_____

_____

_____

_____

_____

"The secret of getting ahead is getting started."

-Mark Twain

10. Motivation is not enough to get you to your goal; action is the only thing that will drive you to achieve your goal. Break your habit of procrastination by making a decision to act on your thoughts now!

_____

_____

_____

_____

_____

_____

_____

_____

_____

_____

_____

_____

_____

_____

_____

_____

_____

"You need to recognize that the risk of moving toward your dreams is much lower than the slow, everyday punishment you inflict on yourself by suppressing your dream."

-Mel Robbins

"I think sometimes in life the biggest challenges end up being the best things that happen in your life."

-Tom Brady

11. This new journey requires a leap of faith within you; do not fear what is going to happen next. Believe in yourself and that anything in life is a possibility, the universe has your back!

_____

_____

_____

_____

_____

_____

_____

_____

_____

_____

_____

_____

_____

_____

_____

_____

_____

"I was always told that I was too small, too skinny, too slow, not tough enough, and I never believed what people told me."

-Joe Theismann

12. Your goal should not be that you want to be better than anyone else, but rather you should strive to be a better version of what you used to be.

_____

_____

_____

_____

_____

_____

_____

_____

_____

_____

_____

_____

_____

_____

_____

_____

_____

_____

"No one can give you heart. No one can give you discipline. No one can make you unstoppable. Those are the things you must decide for yourself. But make no mistake, it's a decision. It's not a genetic gift. It's a mindset."

—————

-Tom Bilyeu

"We first make our habits and then our habits make us!"

-John Dryden

13. Smile, be grateful, laugh, enjoy each day. Show gratitude, love, appreciation, kindness, grace, forgiveness, not only today but each day of your life.

_____

_____

_____

_____

_____

_____

_____

_____

_____

_____

_____

_____

_____

_____

_____

_____

_____

_____

_____

"We are what we repeatedly do, excellence, then, is not an act, but a habit!"

-Aristotle

14. You will never know your limits until you push yourself to them.

_____

_____

_____

_____

_____

_____

_____

_____

_____

_____

_____

_____

_____

_____

_____

_____

_____

_____

_____

_____

"You were born to win, but to be a winner, you must plan to win, prepare to win, and expect to win."

-Zig Ziglar

"You are what you are and where you are because of what's gone into your mind. You can change what you are and where you are by changing what goes into your mind!"

-Zig Ziglar

15. Life is too short not to be doing what you LOVE; break the rules. Forgive quickly, kiss slowly, love truly, laugh uncontrollably and never REGRET anything that makes you smile.

_____

_____

_____

_____

_____

_____

_____

_____

_____

_____

_____

_____

_____

_____

_____

_____

_____

_____

_____

"The greatest discovery of my generation is that human beings can alter their lives by altering their attitudes!"

-William James

16. Make your dreams your new addiction with every breath you take to make everything you are shooting for a reality. Have no plan B; with hard work, commitment and dedication you will succeed.

_____

_____

_____

_____

_____

_____

_____

_____

_____

_____

_____

_____

_____

_____

_____

_____

_____

_____

_____

I came from the bottom of the bottom. It's hard for a lot of people to comprehend my story—a lot of people just don't get me because they haven't experienced it. I came from the bottom and I have risen up and I have changed but never forgotten."

-50 Cent

"There are three types of people in the world. Those who don't know what happened, those who wonder what happened, and people like us from the streets that make things happen.

-Dr.Dre

17. Remember that home is not the shell you climb into every day; it's the people who are there for you, through the good times, through the bad times. Remember to always leave your door open, even when you are at your worst.

_____

_____

_____

_____

_____

_____

_____

_____

_____

_____

_____

_____

_____

_____

_____

_____

"Life's a test, mistakes are lessons, but the gift of life is knowing that you have made a difference."

-Tupac Shakur

18. Never be afraid to fall or fail, those falls or failures teach us life lessons, we grow from them, we learn from them. We truly evolve from all of life's lessons!

_____

_____

_____

_____

_____

_____

_____

_____

_____

_____

_____

_____

_____

_____

_____

_____

_____

_____

"Death is not the greatest loss in life. The greatest loss is what dies inside while still alive. Never surrender."

-Tupac Shakur

"Everybody can be great because anybody can serve. You don't have to have a college degree to serve. You don't have to make your subject and verb agree to serve. You only need a heart full of grace. A soul generated by love!"

-Dr. Martin Luther King, Jr.

19. One of the greatest things I have learned in my life is that you don't get in life what you want! You get in life what you fight for! Never be scared to be yourself, it's okay to be different.

"You miss 100% of the shots you don't take!"

-Wayne Gretzky

20. You must always learn from the past, evaluate what has occurred in your life, so you can apply what you have learned.

_____

_____

_____

_____

_____

_____

_____

_____

_____

_____

_____

_____

_____

_____

_____

_____

_____

_____

_____

"I am intense I am obsessed I do what others refuse to I must control my destiny I am never satisfied I rise while others sleep I refuse to quit I am driven to succeed I am a role model for others."

-Grant Cardone

"Never was anything great achieved without danger."

-Nicola Machiavelli

21. Never form opinions of others or put people down, we honestly do not know the reality of what she or he is going through.

_____

_____

_____

_____

_____

_____

_____

_____

_____

_____

_____

_____

_____

_____

_____

_____

_____

_____

_____

_____

_____

"Be impeccable with your word, don't take anything person-ally, don't make assumptions, always do your best."

-Don Miguel Ruiz

22. Never take anything said to you or done to you personally.

_____

_____

_____

_____

_____

_____

_____

_____

_____

_____

_____

_____

_____

_____

_____

_____

_____

_____

_____

_____

"Strength does not come from winning. Your struggles develop your strengths. When you go through hardships and decide not to surrender, that is strength."

-Arnold Schwarzenegger

"Never confuse movement with progress. Because you can run in place and not get anywhere."

-Denzel Washington

23. Coming to terms with the fact that most people will lie to you is a part of life, they are afraid that you will see right through them. They put on a mask to hide their faults and insecurities because they are scared to death to allow anyone to see them for who they truly are.

_____

_____

_____

_____

_____

_____

_____

_____

_____

_____

_____

_____

_____

_____

_____

_____

"If you don't have the mental capacity to be that obsessed about what you're trying to get... Then MotherFucker you ain't never gonna have it."

-CT Fletcher

24. The only thing we have that is truly ours is our word; practice always being impeccable, even if it hurts to be truthful.

"As long as you are alive, you will either live to accomplish your own goals and dreams or be used as a resource to accomplish someone else's."

-**Grant Cardone**

"You don't have to be great to get started, but you have to get started to be great."

-Les Brown

25. Opinions are nothing but people's points of view; they are not truths and should never be taken to heart.

_____

_____

_____

_____

_____

_____

_____

_____

_____

_____

_____

_____

_____

_____

_____

_____

_____

_____

_____

"Your dream was given to you. If someone else can't see it for you, that's fine, it was given to you and not them. It's your dream, hold it. Nourish it. Cultivate it!"

-Les Brown

26. Every day is a new opportunity to be happy, to be free, to be self-aware and to be awake.

_____

_____

_____

_____

_____

_____

_____

_____

_____

_____

_____

_____

_____

_____

_____

_____

_____

"I don't know what you're up against. I don't know what you're facing. But here's what I do know: You've got something special, you've got greatness in you, and I know it's possible that you can live your dream."

-Les Brown

"No matter your position, circumstances, or opportunities in life, you always have the freedom of mind to choose how you experience, interpret, and, ultimately, shape your world."

-Brendon Burchard

27. The key to financial freedom is not working for your money but rather having your money work for you.

_____

_____

_____

_____

_____

_____

_____

_____

_____

_____

_____

_____

_____

_____

_____

_____

"We do not need magic to change the world; we carry all the power we need inside ourselves already: we have the power to imagine better."

-J.K. Rowling

28. Be in creation, build your own empire, seek out your dreams, it all starts with you and believing in yourself.

"The greatest moments in life are not concern with selfish achievements but rather with the things we do for the people we love and esteem."

———————

-Walt Disney

"For every minute you are angry you lose sixty seconds of happiness."

-Ralph Waldo Emerson

29. When you surround yourself with others who have dreams, desires and ambitions, they will help you shift your perspective on achieving your dreams.

_____

_____

_____

_____

_____

_____

_____

_____

_____

_____

_____

_____

_____

_____

_____

_____

_____

_____

"There is nothing more important to true growth than realizing that you are not the voice of the mind—you are the one who hears it."

-Michael A. Singer

30. The Law of Attraction has always been true for me. When we focus on either positive or negative thoughts, we attract positive or negative experiences to our life. Be mindful of what you are spending your time focusing on because you will attract that into your life.

"Reality has its own power—you can turn your back on it, but it will find you in the end, and your inability to cope with it will be your ruin."

———

-50 Cent

"The future belongs to those who learn more skills and combine them in creative ways."

-Robert Greene

31. The past has already happened; the future has not been written yet. Stop dwelling on things that already happened or things that have not happened. The only control you have is of what is going on with your life right now.

_____

_____

_____

_____

_____

_____

_____

_____

_____

_____

_____

_____

_____

_____

_____

"If you're walking down the right path and you're willing to keep walking, eventually you'll make progress."

-President Barack Obama

32. We all have challenges in our lives; the way we handle them or resolve them can make us or break us. By shifting your perspective on how you endure and overcome them is a true game changer.

_____

_____

_____

_____

_____

_____

_____

_____

_____

_____

_____

_____

_____

_____

_____

_____

_____

_____

_____

_____

"Fear is the path to the dark side. Anger leads to hate, hate leads to suffering."

-Master Yoda

"You must unlearn what you have learned. You will know good from bad when you are calm, at peace and passive."

-Master Yoda

33. Have you figured out your why? All of us are born with a gift, and when you are able to share that gift with others, that is your purpose in life!

_____

_____

_____

_____

_____

_____

_____

_____

_____

_____

_____

_____

_____

_____

_____

_____

_____

_____

_____

_____

_____

"Do not let anything that happens in life be important enough that you're willing to close your heart over it."

-Michael A. Singer

34. In life sometimes we find ourselves on a road that forces us to choose a path. It's not a wrong path or a right one; it's just a new road. It allows us to reflect on where we've been and where we want to go. It also teaches us what really matters to our soul.

_____

_____

_____

_____

_____

_____

_____

_____

_____

_____

_____

_____

_____

_____

_____

"People see what they want to see and what people want to see never has anything to do with the truth."

-Roberto Bolano

"It is unwise to be sure of one's own wisdom."

-Mahatma Gandhi

35. Our biggest teachers are those who challenge us, push us and are boldly honest with us. They teach us to be humble, to be grateful and to realize that we are not complete.

_____

_____

_____

_____

_____

_____

_____

_____

_____

_____

_____

_____

_____

_____

_____

_____

_____

_____

"When you arise in the morning, think of what a privilege it is to be alive—to breathe, to think, to enjoy, to love."

-Marcus Aurelius

36. Never forget that if you truly love someone you should tell them because hearts are often broken by words that were never spoken.

"When you judge another,
you do not define them,
you define yourself."

-Dr. Wayne Dyer

"The greatest detriment as a leader that you inflict on your success of business is when you put yourself first."

-Simon Sinek

37. Remember that as we close a door in a chapter of our lives, a new door and new opportunities will always unfold.

_____

_____

_____

_____

_____

_____

_____

_____

_____

_____

_____

_____

_____

_____

_____

_____

_____

_____

"Success isn't always about greatness, it's about consistency. Constant hard work gains success. Greatness will come."

-Dwayne "The Rock" Johnson

38. Be humble, be Noblesse, be Courteous, have Largesse, be Loyal, have Prowess, have Valor, be Just, have Honor, be Truthful.

_____

_____

_____

_____

_____

_____

_____

_____

_____

_____

_____

_____

_____

_____

_____

_____

_____

"To achieve anythingyou need a burning desire."

-Napoleon Hill

"If you kick back it's all gone. Continue to attack your goals with intensity & commitment!"

-Lee Labrada

39. "Do your best to be committed to self-development not self-destruction. Anyone or anything that pushes you away from reaching your dreams has to go!" Grant Cardone

_____

_____

_____

_____

_____

_____

_____

_____

_____

_____

_____

_____

_____

_____

_____

_____

_____

"It is amazing how your life changes when you embrace the reality that you're better than the life you've settled for."

-Dr. Steve Maraboli

40. Making time for yourself is one of the biggest challenges you will face. It is important to make time for yourself. We are always doing for others and we forget that we are important too.

_____

_____

_____

_____

_____

_____

_____

_____

_____

_____

_____

_____

_____

_____

_____

_____

_____

_____

"Being positive is actually a choice. It's a choice we all make, to choose positive even in the most negative situations. Of course, it's hard if something negative has happened, or life seems to be against you, but you can still choose to be positive."

-**Dan Nevins**

'It's not how much start you have; it's how much heart you have!"

-James Malinchak

41. Never stop thinking like a 5-year-old. When you are that age, you are always in questioning mode, hyper learning mode, and you have a deep thirst to learn about everything you see and touch.

"A good pilot is compelled to always evaluate what happens so he can apply what he's learned."

-Top Gun "Viper"

42. How can we do something surprising and memorable with our lives? How can we run this job, in small, but important ways into a better representation of ourselves?

"Jerry Maguire Manifesto"

_____

_____

_____

_____

_____

_____

_____

_____

_____

_____

_____

_____

_____

_____

_____

_____

_____

"You become what you believe. You are where you are today in your life based on everything you have believed."

_____

-Oprah Winfrey

"I would like to thank the people who've brought me those dark moments, when I felt most wounded, betrayed. You have been my greatest teachers."

-Oprah Winfrey

43. We are only here on this planet, in this moment, in this body, in this era at this present time. Make each moment count and impact the lives of everyone you meet along the way in a positive way.

_____

_____

_____

_____

_____

_____

_____

_____

_____

_____

_____

_____

_____

_____

_____

_____

_____

_____

"In the end, we will remember not the words of our enemies, but the silence of our friends."

-Dr. Martin Luther King Jr.

44. Life teaches us so many things and if we are open to learn from the lessons we can transform to a higher spiritual level.

_____

_____

_____

_____

_____

_____

_____

_____

_____

_____

_____

_____

_____

_____

_____

_____

_____

"We live in a world of hypocrites, where people pray for your downfall but smile in your face like they love you all at the same time."

_____

-*Joker* Dark Knight

"I'm strong because I've been weak. I'm fearless because I've been afraid. I'm wise because I've been foolish."

-Joker Dark Knight

45. What dream are you chasing? It doesn't matter how old you are, your background, your education, or your past; it all starts with believing in yourself, anything in life is a possibility.

_____

_____

_____

_____

_____

_____

_____

_____

_____

_____

_____

_____

_____

_____

_____

_____

_____

_____

_____

"It doesn't matter who you are. What matters is your plan."

-Tom Hardy

46. Once you start associating pleasure in your grind, your body rewards you with its maximum perfection. Rise up, get up and go out and get what is rightfully yours.

"People should pursue what they're passionate about. That will make them happier than pretty much anything else."

-**Elon Musk**

MEET ALONSO SANCHEZ

I have been working as a professional in the health and fitness field since 1987. As your personal health and fitness consultant, I find that it is my job to educate and advise you on positive lifestyle routines while providing you with an adequate road map to living an active and healthy life. Do not allow yourself to be fooled by mainstream media into thinking that there is a magic pill, routine or diet that will instantly change your body. The only way to achieve your personal fitness goal is through hard work, dedication, and commitment to current self and the future "you". You should always listen to your body, feed it correctly, train daily, and rest, and the changes you are looking for will automatically occur.

Certified by N.A.S.M. / A.C.E. with over 31 years of experience not only as a personal trainer; I have had the opportunity to manage multi-million dollar facilities in Miami, Florida. My clients range from celebrities to stay-at-home moms, professional athletes to business executives. My main focus is the benefits obtained by living a healthy lifestyle, which includes proper nutrition, healthy eating, and correct biomechanics, to ensure a complete training program that benefits you all around.

In my 31 years not only have I trained clients, but I also have had the privilege of training trainers and assisted in trainers' certification programs such as N.A.S.M with Dr. Bob Goldman, Dr. Mark Slavin and Founder Tom Purvis (RPT) with resistance training specialist certification. My unique training style incorporates many different styles of programs, ranging from old-school body building techniques to hit training, TRX, strength and conditioning , circuit training, CrossFit style routines, power yoga, and real weight loss programs to help you obtain your goals.

My journey went from being in the best shape of my life to falling into a deep rabbit hole. I gained 52 lbs of unhealthy weight and my body fat percentage also increased to about 28%. I became addicted to sugar, fat foods, and the worst addiction of all was methylene-dioxymethamphetamine (commonly known as Ecstasy). This combination of foods, sugar and drugs addiction caused me to fall into a dark hole, which I call my rabbit hole.

I attribute my decline to bad choices, car accidents and getting hurt lifting heavy weights. All this put me on a downward spiral, from 1999 to 2014. My dedication to my profession in those 15 years allowed me to function in my everyday activities never missing a day of work or canceling on my clients.

In 2014 I discovered Yoga. This was my first step towards a healthy lifestyle. Yoga was the catalyst that allowed me to heal my inner self through self-awareness, mindfulness and being present. Also, it helped strengthen my core, my joints, my muscles and my ability to move with full range of motion without pain.

Once I achieved this level of being able to move freely without pain I was able to integrate body building techniques, cardiovascular training and a regimen of deep trigger point therapy to promote healthier muscle growth.

The last part of my journey to achieve my transformation was a complete eating lifestyle change, which began in January 2017. I am in the process of writing a complete autobiography of my journey and how I was able to achieve this change.

Last thought, whether you achieve your dreams and goals is solely up to you. From personal experience I can tell you that no one can do it for you and no one can make you a guarantee that you will achieve success. It's all up to you to go out and chase your dreams and don't take no for an answer. To become successful you must have a plan, a strategy; model after others who have achieved what you want. You do not have to reinvent the wheel!

Alonso Sanchez
www.AlonsoSanchez.com
@AlonsoSanchez

Journaling has always helped me look back at my life, on how I was thinking at the moment. Here is some space for you to reflect and commit to yourself.